Carlow
in old picture postcards volume 2

by Michael Purcell

European Library ZALTBOMMEL/ THE NETHERLANDS

To my special friend Hollie Conville, B.B.

IRL ISBN 90 288 1526 0

© 1999 European Library – Zaltbommel/The Netherlands

Introduction

In the introduction to volume one of 'Carlow in old picture postcards' I gave a fairly comprehensive history of Carlow town. I intend to use this introduction to volume two as an index to all of the pictures published in both volumes.

Sharon Grant is employed by Carlow County Heritage Society on a FÁS C.E. Training Scheme. I thank Sharon for her advice and for typing up my scribbled notes. Also I appreciate the financial aid I received from Sam McCauley's chemist and photo bar towards reproduction costs of some of the postcards in this volume.

1 A short walk from Carlow town we have Browneshill Dolmen or Portal Tomb, erected sometime between 4000 and 3000BC. The area has not been excavated so we know little about it. In the picture we can see the two portal stones with the gate stone in the centre supporting the capstone which weighs about 100 metric tonnes. It is in the care of Duchas, The Heritage Service, a Government agency responsible for National Monuments and Historic Sites.

2   Built in 1763 overlooking Carlow town, Brownes' Hill House was home to the Browne family, gentry landlords, who came to Ireland in 1650 from Buckinghamshire, England. During the War of Independence 1918-1921, Robert Browne Clayton had a machine gun placed on the roof of the house, loaded and ready for action in case of attack from the Irish Republican Army (I.R.A.). Through intermarriage the family became known as Browne Clayton and Clayton Browne. The following pictures introduce us to two members of the family circa 1875.

3 Mr. Browne Clayton – Mr. Clayton Browne. For further information on the gentry families of Carlow read 'The Carlow Gentry' by Jimmy O'Toole.

Mr Browne Clayton.

Mr Clayton Browne.

4 The ruins of one stately mansion, Duckett's Grove, built circa 1790 as the home of the Duckett family. It was destroyed by fire in 1933. Ten years earlier the contents of the house had been auctioned off. It was uninhabited at the time of the fire. During 'the troubles' the building was used as a headquarters by the I.R.A. The period 1919-1923 came to be known as 'the troubles' covering the War of Independence and the devastating Civil War that followed.

5 ... *their marching and drilling, awoke in the glenside sounds awesome and thrilling.* Volunteers on parade at Ducketts Grove. At the time this picture was taken Liam Stack (see picture number 41) was officer-in-charge of the I.R.A. forces in Carlow. The statuary visible in the background was used for target practice by the volunteers.

6 Braganza Villa, named after the ruling family of Portugal, was designed by Thomas Cobden. It was built for Dudley Hill, Secretary to the Grand Jury of Carlow. The first stone was laid in 1819 and the building was completed in 1823. From the Carlow Post of July 1823 we read: 'To be let, for any term that may be agreed on, the elegant and modern built commodious House of Braganza.' In 1826 the residence was purchased for Dr. James Doyle, Bishop of Kildare and Leighlin. It remained the residence of all the succeeding bishops up to the death on 22 May 1969 of Bishop Thomas Keogh. The house standing on seven acres of land was sold for £22,000 by public auction in July 1972. This picture of Braganza House is from the Lawrence Collection of photographs.

In volume one with picture number 26 of 'Carlow in old picture postcards' I outlined the history of the Lawrence Collection.

7 Situated on the outskirts of Carlow town, Ballykealy House was designed by Thomas Cobden for John J. Lecky. Styled in the Tudor revival architecture it was built circa 1830. It was acquired by the religious order of Patrician Brothers in 1962 and used as a novitiate by them for many years. It was sold in 1980 and reopened in 1988 as Ballykealy House Hotel.

8   Borris House, situated a short distance from Carlow town is the residence of the Mc Murrough Kavanagh family, descendants of the Kings of Leinster. This picture was taken by Iona Mac Leod. Iona was Carlow County Librarian 1930 to 1971 and was a generous supporter of many local artists and voluntary groups. Carlow County Heritage Society have erected a plaque to her memory. Iona died in December 1998 and following her death I inherited her large collection of photographs and slides. In June 1999 Iona's art collection was auctioned to raise funds for the Holy Angels Day Care Centre. I am grateful to Nurse Geraldine Connell, administrator of the centre for her help in compiling this volume.

9   On the outskirts of the town we have this view of the arched entrance gates to Oak Park, the estate of the Bruen family. The arch was designed by William Morrison in 1833 and included living accommodation for the gatekeeper and his family. We can see the edge of the cast-iron gates on each side. Oak Park was taken over by the Agricultural Institute in 1961. The land was divided, some of it was acquired by the Carlow Rugby Football Club.

10   A lady in a boat on the river Barrow paddles contentedly past Belmont House on the Kilkenny Road. Belmont was demolished in 1972. Today the newly-erected Dolmen Hotel stands on the site. Noted for its personal touch and high standards, the management have incorporated into the running of the hotel the elegance and comfort that was so much part of life when Belmont House and Estate flourished. At the turn of the century Belmont was owned by Captain Jocelyn Henry Watkins Thomas. From the Carlow Vestry Register of 1788, we learn that *Captain Jocelyn Davidson Esq. died on 8th September aged 78 and was buried at so early an hour as 1 o'clock in the morning beneath the Cedars in the Burial Field at Old Derrig.* This was the private burial ground of the Thomas family of Belmont.

11 Some of the employ-
ees of Belmont Estate circa 1900. Note the lady with
the shawl and hat.

12   From the group in the previous picture we have herself, here in a clay pipe puffing pose; a woman pipe smoker was a common enough sight at the turn of the century. All we know for sure is that she was the vegetable gardener for the big house and it is said she came from Myshall, County Carlow. The Belmont photos are courtesy of Mary Slattery, Kilkenny Road, Carlow.

13 In 1847 Knockbeg the mansion home of the Carruther family was purchased by Dr. James Taylor, President of St. Patrick's Seminary. It was used as a preparatory school for 8-12 year old boys. Around the time this picture was taken Knockbeg had become a lay college and was known as St. Mary's. Today Knockbeg is a valued educational institution and has prepared thousands of students for roles in all walks of life.

14 This five-photo card is postmarked 1960. The message on the back reads: *Dear Peg, Carlow is one of the cleanest towns in Ireland with wonderful people, making it a pleasant place to stay. I was out in Killeshin yesterday and had a great drinking day. Wish you were here, Joe.*
All of the scenes pictured have been covered in volume one of 'Carlow in old picture postcards'.

15 This aerial postcard from 1959 gives us a good view of Carlow Courthouse and surrounds. The field to the rear of the Courthouse is now a link road with houses, car park and the new Garda Station built on the area. Many of the other sites are easily identifiable.

16 This earlier view gives us a good look at the top of the Courthouse and surrounds.

We see a cart outside Nelson's Fruit and Vegetable shop, a man in a white apron stands at the door of the Irishman's pub and Stathams Garage is under construction.

The pupils of the C.B.S. Academy in College Street are playing in the school yard. Only four cars are visible

17 Pupils from the Christian Brothers school put on a gymnastics display in the grounds of St. Dympna's Hospital, circa 1930's.

18 The Bishop Foley Primary School was open in 1938. This Slógagh award winning picture was taken by Rory Óg Mórán. The school was run by the Christian Brother religious community.

19 Christian Brothers pose with two past pupils. The Brothers took great pride in the achievements of their past pupils. Today, due to the drop in vocations, the Bishop Foley school is staffed entirely by lay teachers. Pictured here are, standing left to right: Brother P.C. Lenihan, Br. P.C. Tracy, Br.O. Kenny, Br. E.Rodgers and Br. D. O'Neill. Front row: Fr. Finn, Brother K. Moore and Fr. Johnson.

20 This is a rare view of Carlow Cathedral. A cruciform building designed by Thomas Cobden, it was completed in 1833. The front yard is dug up and in the porch to the left we see a framed notice in the hall, this was a list of people who were entitled to use the gallery and transepts in the Cathedral. This picture was taken by Leo O'Brien around 1935, and is remarkable for the time because it was photographed with a box camera. The view covers over 150 feet and includes the top of the railings to the top of the lantern tower.

21 Another unusual picture of the Cathedral with a scene that has disappeared from the Carlow landscape. Seven nuns of the Religious Order of the Presentation teaching community relax in a contemplative pose in their private garden. The huge tree to the right covers the burial ground of the sisters, in use since they were established in Carlow in 1810. The statue in the centre of the picture was a favourite background with generations of Carlovians for First Communion, Confirmation and wedding photographs. Today the once beautiful gardens are gone, replaced by houses, offices and our new County Library. The Presentation nuns remain involved in teaching and community work in Carlow.

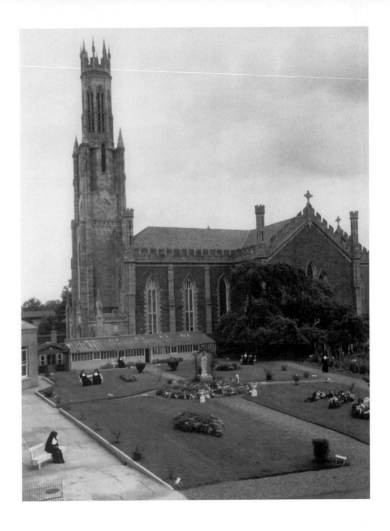

22 Twenty-seven Presentation sisters pictured outside the convent, they are known only by the name they have taken in religious life. Front row, left to right: Sister Brigid, Sr. Therese, Sr. Colmcille, Sr. Conleth, Sr. Philomena, Sr. Rosario, Sr. Albeus and Sr. Lazerian. Middle row: Sr. Cecilia, Sr. Brigida, Sr. Killian, Sr. Columba, Sr. Pius, Sr. Gerard, Sr. Assumpta, Sr. Patricia, Sr. Frances Xavier, Sr. Oliver and Sr. Dolores. Back row: Sr. Dympna, Sr. Madeleine, Sr. Catherine, Sr. Emmanuel, Sr. Veronica, Sr. Canice, Sr. Agnes and Sr. Paul.

23 In this view of upper Tullow Street we see Dinty Delaney's pub on the left. Painted on the front wall is 'The Old House', it is now the 'Med' bar. Alongside we see the Presentation Convent. On our right the Munster and Leinster Bank, above that a man wheels a hand truck to carry a delivery from the horse and dray, while the driver holds the horse. The house in the distance facing the camera is Noud's grocery and post office.

24 Formerly Bolger's Hotel, this building was later owned by Patrick Lawler, who operated a bacon-curing business and a wine and spirit store. At the time this picture was taken it was the Munster and Leinster Bank. Later the bank was demolished and replaced by a new bank built to the rear of the building. In 1973 the Munster & Leinster Bank amalgamated with the Provincial Bank of Ireland to become Allied Irish Bank.

25 The doorway on the left leads to the private quarters of the bank (previous picture), the shop alongside is Walsh's drapery and beside that is the shop of Nicholas Roche. He claimed that he had the cheapest house in Leinster for motor cars, motor lorries and motor cycles. Nicholas was a noted cyclist and a member of the Urban District Council. Today both shops are amalgamated, forming Darcy's shop, furniture and floor covering supplies. The next building, recessed from the streetline, is the Garda Barracks. The scrolled sign on the adjoining wall advertises Finegan's grocery and public house.

26 Drawn by a gas-powered tractor, a barge is transported from Thompson's Engineering Works to be launched on the river Barrow. The man on the right of the barge is John Reynolds, the three men on the left side are John Kennedy, Ned Walker and Pat Condron. At the door of Finegan's we see Pat Finegan. Two messenger bikes are parked, one belongs to Toomey's grocery and the other to Hearns's butcher shop.

27 To the immediate right of the picture we can see a corner of the pointed doorway which leads to the Y.M.C.A. recreation hall, beside that is No. 135, Colgans stationery, toys and newsagency shop. It is such a long shot of lower Tullow street that space does not permit me to name each shop individually. To the left of the picture we see Hadden's Drapery Stores. The house and shop facing us at the end of the street belong to Michael Byrne, bacon curer and lard refiner, and is situated at the Market Cross.

Tullow Street, Carlow.

28 Number 7 Tullow Street, Dan McDonnell's was better known as Buzz's. This early 19th century shopfront is long gone and is replaced with a modern exterior. It has re-opened as a public house with entertainment and restaurant facilities and is officially named 'Buzz's'. The McDonnell family owned several pubs and a grocery shop in Carlow and were active in politics.

29   Coming to the west end of the south side of lower Tullow Street, we can see the last three letters of the name Douglas over Number 5. A watchmaker and jeweller, he also sold gramophones and gramophone records. The building adjoining Douglas is the drapers shop of Thomas Murphy at 2, 3 and 4 Tullow Street. The shopfront contains the first large plate glass windows installed in Carlow. Next door, with the bicycles and hardware merchandise on the footpath, is Willie Mulhall's. Today Paul's bookshop occupies the premises. Note the cast iron cresting on the shop front.

The area beside Mulhall's is known as the Market Cross and across the street can be seen the end portion of Governey's Boot shop in Castle Street, with Miss Murphy's hairdressing salon next door.

30 With the plate glass windows intact, Melville's replaced Thomas Murphy's drapery in the previous picture. Opened on 15th November 1957, the shop overflowed with customers for 'the sales' during the following three days. The opening sale had been advertised for weeks with the promise of 'Small Profits, Quick Returns', also promising to 'clip close on overheads, so that we can shave close on profits'. With branches in Dundalk, Drogheda, Longford and Dublin, the manager of the Carlow branch was Tom Nicholson.

31 Moving down the street we see on the left the railings which encloses a farm machinery display belonging to Gillespie's, who replaced Mulhall's hardware (picture number 29). We get a better view of Governey's boot shop and to our right we see a portion of Duggan's grocery shop.

32   On the north side of Tullow Street, we have this 1928 view of the Arcade ladies outfitters and haberdashery. A corner shop, the section on the right is in Tullow Street, the section facing us is in Dublin Street. The adjoining shop No. 1 Dublin Street, established in 1900, belonged to John and Ellen O'Neill. They sold their own fresh garden produce, vegetables, fruit and flowers. Their son John and his wife Margaret O'Neill later established a fish shop here. Beside O'Neills is No. 2 – McGrath's Medical Hall.

33 Turning the camera to the left of the previous picture, we get this clear view of the remainder of Dublin Street in 1906. On the lantern we can read 'McGrath'. Dan McGrath was the owner of the Carlow Medical Hall. Note the huge pair of spectacles hanging over the door at Number 6. Way down the street two men on extremely long ladders lean against the National Bank, 43 Dublin Street. Three young boys and a girl study the photographer. Note the plus-fours on the boy (right), and the size of the hat on the girl (left) in the donkey and trap. It seems to be a warm sunny afternoon (all of the windows in Duggan's are open), yet those pictured appear to be heavily dressed.

34 Aerial view of Dublin Street and lower Tullow Street. On the lower right, an x marks the area outlined in the previous three pictures. Note the sidewalk display of machinery beside Gillespie's hardware shop.

35 This picture speaks for itself, Carlow post office in Dublin Street. To the right of the picture we catch a glimpse of the entrance. The office moved to Burrin Street in 1968.

36 This rare picture of Dublin Street was taken circa 1895, before the Provincial Bank building was erected. Also we see the old style Duggan's shop before the new shop-front was added. All the shop windows are shuttered, this practice of shuttering was continued on many shops up to the 1970's. The last to put up wooden shutters was Charlie Lewis in Dublin Street.

37 This boot and shoe re-
pair shop remained in the
same family for three generations. Pictured is Charlie
Lewis, who died aged 49
in 1931. His son Charlie
carried on the business. He
died aged 75 years in
1994.

38 At Coleman's Garage we see Tommy Dooley at the petrol pumps. Numerous shop signs can be seen, McNally Chemist, Sugar Bowl Café, post office, Ewing's Restaurant. A library sign dominates Cigar Divan. Also in the picture B.P. Oil, Cunningham's Ladies and Gents Hairdressing, McElwee's newsagent, Paddy Kinsella's Radio Shop, Oliver's Butchers and the Royal Hotel.

39 A front view of Colemans at the turn of the century. Note the motorized Quadro Cycle. This cycle is still in use today and is a major attraction at motor vintage shows throughout the country. Colemans continue to trade at 19 and 20 Dublin Street. The business, remaining in the same family for over two hundred years, is one of the oldest established family concerns in Ireland.

40   Dublin Street – many of the houses have flags flying for An Tóstal celebrations 1953. The house on the right is the office and home of solicitor Hugh O'Donnell, next door with the steps is the office and home of architect Godfrey McDonald, next is the Vogue hairdressing salon run by Irene Burke. On our left we see the house of Aidan Walsh, veterinary surgeon, with Mr. Tucker's dentist surgery next door. The next house is the home of Dr. Larry Doyle, who served as Dispensary Doctor from 1913 to 1958. The two ladies are Teasie Colclough Brennan and her daughter Kathleen.

41 At No. 44 Dublin Street, Francis McAnally owned this pharmaceutical and dispensing chemist shop, oculist's prescriptions and spectacles were also supplied. Unfortunately, this shop front was replaced in 1953 with a modern exterior. During the War of Independence a man known as Liam Leahy worked here as a chemist's assistant. Leahy was the undercover name used by Liam Stack, who was the officer-in-charge of the local Irish Republican Army Units. Liam married local girl Sarah Reynolds of the Courthouse. Later he was promoted to the rank of Chief Superintendent in the newly-formed police force, the Garda Síochána.

42 Women played an important role during the War of Independence and the Civil War. Lena Whelan of the Dublin Road is pictured here in her Cumann na mBan (Women's Army) uniform. The bandolier belonged to Tom Seely of Tullow Street, who was active in the I.R.A. movement. In 1997 Carlow County Heritage Society returned the bandolier to Tom's grandson Fintan Seely, who is a well-known New York publican. It is now on display in his pub in Manhattan. My own mother was in Cumann na mBan and in 1923 she was interred in Kilmainham Jail. In 1927 Lena Whelan married Dick Clifford, an ex-British Army soldier. This postcard came to me courtesy of Lena's niece Catherine Smith of Smith's newsagency.

43 With the country still in a state of unrest, soldiers of the newly-established Free State Army parade in the Haymarket in 1923. From here they marched to the Old Union Workhouse on the Kilkenny Road which had been converted to a barracks. In the background the gates lead to the Buttermarket and Carlow Fire Station at the rear of the Town Hall.

44 The rear of the old Union Workhouse following its conversion into an army barracks. It was found to be unsuitable and within a short time was handed over to Carlow County Council for use as offices and stores. It was demolished in 1971. Carlow's Regional College, Institute of Technology, now stands on the site.

45 Sunday after last Mass, with the Cathedral in the background. Carlovians drill and parade in the barrack yard. Ireland remained neutral during the Second World War and despite the fact that there were not enough weapons to arm the National Army, local citizens joined the L.D.F. (Local Defence Force), and prepared to repel 'invasion from any quarter'.

46 'The Mighty Judge Ascends.' Two trumpeters sound the Royal Salute on Monday, 16th July 1906 at 11 a.m. as the Right Honourable Mr. Justice Andrews arrives at Carlow Courthouse to open the Summer Assizes. On his left is High Sheriff Sir Francis Denys, behind him comes the judge's crier carrying his staff. A squad of R.I.C. men form a guard of honour. Under the lantern on the right stands District Inspector S. Carter with his distinctive Kaiser moustache. Members of the gentry look on, later they will form the Grand Jury. The judge represented the Crown and from the time of his arrival at the railway station he was treated with great respect. The judge usually stayed in Misses Spongs' establishment on the Kilkenny Road, from there he was escorted to the courthouse by a *troop of groomed and resplendent cavalry.* After the ceremony the troops and constabulary adjourned for food and porter to Turk Murphy's canteen in Barrack Street.

47 With St. Anne's Protestant Memorial Church, Athy Road in the background, a little boy stands alone in the middle of the quarry that adjoins the 'Old Graves'. For many years this area was used as the town dump. It was levelled and landscaped and in 1953 was opened as the town park. Later the town outdoor swimming pool was located here. Renamed Shaw Park there are now modern homes built on the site.

ST. ANNE'S CHURCH. CARLOW. 7513.

48 St. Anne's pictured in 1920. The interior re-mained much the same following its re-erection in Graiguecullen in 1928. The building was purchased by the Catholic Church au-thorities from the Church of Ireland community for a nominal sum. Having dis-mantled and numbered each stone, local people carted the church over the river Barrow, where it be-came St. Clare's Roman Catholic Parish Church of Graiguecullen.

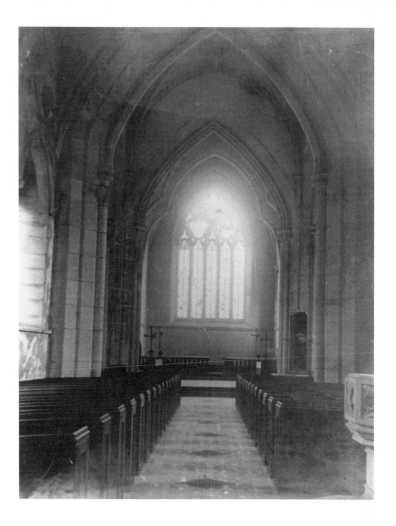

49 Sixteen members of the Poor Clare enclosed order of nuns pose for this picture circa 1940. The order came to Graiguecullen in 1893. They have practised perpetual adoration day and night continuously since 1903. Their convent is attached to St. Clare's Church.

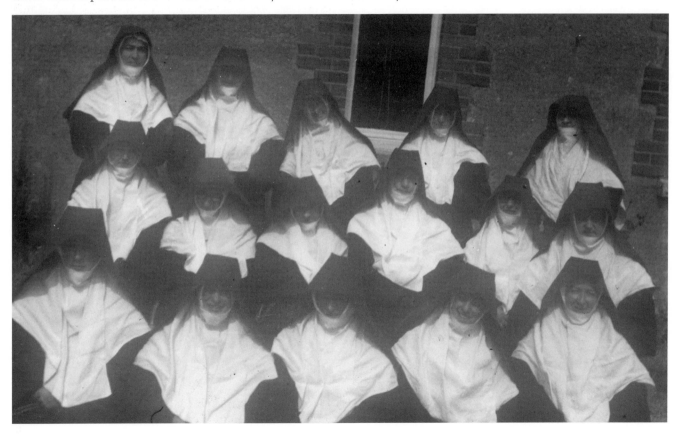

50 A barge being loaded at Shackelton's Mills, pictured from the island at Websters Lock. To the left of the picture we see the lock-keeper, Michael Webster. In 1898 Michael was presented with a purse of sovereigns and a special commendation certificate:

In appreciation of the gallant life-saving services rendered by Michael Webster who, from time to time rescued from drowning, at great personal risk, some 29 lives.

It was signed by seventy-four prominent citizens of Carlow.

51   On the right of this picture we can just about see the Minister for Industry and Commerce, Mr. Sean Lemass (marked x). He is present on 21st January 1935 to perform the official opening of the Barrow Mills, Graiguecullen. He watches as four priests assist the seventy-year-old Bishop Matthew Cullen with the blessing ceremony. The mills were constructed and modernized by Alfred Little who, along with his fellow directors Edward Duggan and A.P. Coleman, created much-needed employment in difficult times by investing in the industry. Within twelve months of the events pictured below Bishop Cullen was dead.

52 It looks as if the whole population of Graiguecullen village turned out for the opening of the Barrow Mills. Five Mass servers lead Fr. P. MacSuibhne, Bishop Cullen and Fr. J. Fogarty, whilst Fr. J. Campion and Fr. T. Burbage flank Minister Sean Lemass on the way to St. Clare's Church after the blessing ceremony. To the right we see the old R.I.C. Barracks with houses to the rear built in 1867 by Rowan McCombe, Superintendent of the Barrow Navigation Company.

53 A very early picture of the River Barrow. To the left, on the Graiguecullen side of the river, we see the Barrow Navitation Company Stores with two docks for barges. In 1990 all this area was demolished and cleared and is being developed as a community park. 'X' marks the stables belonging to the National Bank, situated in the 'Bank field', where in later years carnivals were held. It is now a carpark. The spire of St. Anne's Church on the Athy Road can be seen in the background.

RIVER BARROW, CARLOW.

54 Looking in the opposite direction of the previous picture we see the Killeshin hills in the background. A lone figure watches as three men in a boat move down the river. Seemingly Carlow Rowing Club is already established in the light-coloured building on the left. The club purchased the Canal Stores in March 1961 and after extensive refurbishment the new clubhouse opened in 1962. The large building in the background was built in the early nineteenth century as the Flyboat Hotel to cater for boat passengers.

55   In this 1953 picture of Coal Market flags fly from several houses to mark An Tóstal. On the left we see Michael Murphy standing outside the public house owned by his father Frank. Next door is Broughans hardware store. I was born in the street but space does not permit me to name the families who lived in each house. On the left is Walshe's stonecutters with tombstones on display behind the railings. Next are Gillespie's stores with trailers parked outside. In the background we see the tower of the Cathedral and the spire of St. Mary's Church. The picture was taken on a Thursday afternoon. At that time all the business premises closed for half-day on Thursday, that is why the street looks so quite.

56 With M.S. (Munster Sims) petrol pumps added to Broughan's hardware store we have Mister Musicman Michael Foley standing beside one of the pumps. Michael was a dance band leader and in later years supplied musical instruments and equipment to the trade. Beside Michael we see Neddy Broughan with the ever present cigarette cupped in his hand. He was known to everyone as 'Neighbour Broughan'. The small boy is Paddy Munnelly with meself standing next to him, next to me is Neddy's wife Maggie. Neddy and Maggie are a happy part of the vista of my youth. It seemed to me that Maggie never stopped talking, with Neddy, in the background repeating over and over 'for God's sake Maggie would you ever stay quite'. However, when Maggie died in November 1965 Neddy's true feelings came to the surface, it was then, for the first time I saw a grown man cry.

57 Across the road from Broughan's we get this view of John Street, the playground for all the youth of the area. Gillespie's stores are on the right. The first of the tall buildings at the end of the street is Gracie Fenlons, with Donoghue's 'haunted house' next door. The cart outside of Donoghue's belongs to the O'Brien family, who came from India and had many exciting stories to tell of life outside of Ireland and their travels across the world.

58 A scene we hope is gone forever. Residents of John Street battle against the river Barrow as the floods rise. Pictured are members of the Dunny family outside of their house, this is the house that later became known to us as Donoghue's. It was in fact part of the property given to the people of Carlow by George Bernard Shaw. Across the road in Ballymanus Terrace we see O'Neill the boatsman with his horse and cart reversed to the front of his house as he prepares to move to higher ground. Note the water pump in the centre of the picture.

59 The welted department in Governey's Boot Factory in 1914. The boots on the centre rack were known as the Glace Kid Derby Leather Lined Goodyear Welted Boot. They sold for twelve shillings (60 pence). The Catherlogh Castle Boot Factory was established in 1903 by Michael Governey. He had been looking around for suitable employment opportunities for women and following his attendance at an exhibition in Cork city, he came back to Carlow with the idea of opening a boot and shoe factory. At its peak the factory manufactured 4,000 pairs a week and employed four hundred people. Posters displayed throughout Ireland stated: 'North, South, East and West, Governey's Shoes are the best'.

60　Governey's had their own retail outlet in Carlow town situated at the Market Cross. In 1993 the building was demolished and re-built and is now First Active Building Society. The man pictured at the shop door is Joe Hosey of Castle Hill. He worked for Governey's for nearly sixty years and was a collector for church funds and many other charitable causes. To the left we see the corner of Gaffney's shop in Burrin Street which features in the next picture.

61 Nabbed: with catapult and sling in hand and broken window in centre, young O'Brien has his name taken by Garda Denis Flynn. The shop is Gaffney's in Burrin Street, located in previous picture. Note the display in the shop window, and the sign advertising a G.A.A. 7 a-side in the Gaelic Grounds, Carlow. I gave a brief account of the service record of Garda Flynn in volume 1, number 28. This award-winning picture was taken by Leo O'Brien in the 1930's. Leo's collection of photographs has never been traced. I would like to hear from readers who may have information on same.

62 Portion of Burrin Street – on the right Foyle's library sign marks the entrance to O'Neill's newsagents, next door is Watchorn's fruit and vegetable shop. Left of the picture we see Gillespie's shop having extended their premises to incorporate Gaffney's shop, the Irish Transport and General Workers Union (I.T.G.W.U.) headquarters is next door, the next two shops are Quinn's grocery, provision and confectionery shop. The new post office is not yet built and probably is at construction stage as seen in picture number 65.

63   This very special photo was given to me by Godfrey F. McDonald of Dublin Street. Godfrey recognized the importance of the photo when he studied picture number 52 in volume 1 of 'Carlow in old picture postcards'. The picture was photographed from alongside the Deighton Hall on Tuesday, 7th October 1906 following the Burrin Street fire. Members of the volunteer fire brigade Dick Rogers and Pat O'Toole stand centre picture with shovels in hand; also looking towards the camera is the man who it is thought deliberately started the fire. Note the fire hose box to the right. Carlow post office stands on the site today.

64 This is the only picture of the interior of Frank Slater's cinema. The cinema was built in 1913 on the burnt-out site in the previ-ous picture. With the big screen behind them the talented youth of Carlow assemble on stage for the 1928 Christmas Panto-mime. Sean Prendergast is marked x, his younger brother Pearse stands on his right. The two musical directors signed the post-card, they were Mary M. Whyte and Gwyndolyn L. Williams. The cinema was destroyed by fire on 27th December 1937.

65 The same location as picture number 63 but taken sixty years later. The telephone exchange is already erected, work is in progress building the new post office, the new road is in use though not yet named President J.F. Kennedy Avenue, in the background we see the remains of the last of the Bridewell Lane houses. I think the photographer is Donal Godfrey, one of the great visual recorders of the Carlow landscape. Donal died on 25th December 1969, his collection of photographs forms a wonderful archive and is an important resource for historians.

66 Carlow's first car crash? No one was hurt when the wheel came off this number 9 car near Gurteen Cross on the road from Castledermot to Carlow. The driver was taking part in the 1903 Gordon Bennett Race which passed through Carlow. A special Act of Parliament was passed to close certain Irish roads for the race. Hundreds of R.I.C. constables were on duty, at least half a dozen of them are pictured at this scene.

67 This picture affords us a rare view of Carlow Gas Works which was situated at the end of Montgomery Street (now Greenvale Bacon factory). William Brennan of Bridewell Lane worked here all his life. This picture is courtesy of his grandson Willie Brennan of Graiguecullen. The Carlow Gaslight Company was established in 1846. The site pictured above was leased to the Gas Company by Francis Malcolmson. The large building to the left was formerly Mr. Bewley's textile factory and later it was used as a malthouse by the Kane Brothers. The area was at a lower level than most of the town and was, we are told, ideally suited for distributing gas. The supply ceased in 1956 when the works closed.

68   Greenbank House, Athy Road was the home of the Haughton family. Later Michael Molloy M.P. lived here. At the time this picture was taken it had become the Crofton Hotel and was a popular entertainment venue in the town. The entrance pictured above was formerly the cellar, but the ground was lowered in the 1960's to add another storey to the hotel. Today it is the Seven Oaks Hotel, noted for its personal management, hospitality and quality service and accommodation.

Crofton Hotel, Athy Road, Carlow.
Telephone 288.

69   Bishop Patrick Foley and Mr. Neermaun on the site for the 'beet factory' in 1926. Of course it was a sugar factory but from the beginning it has always been called the beet factory. A few months after this picture was taken Bishop Foley died, on 24th July 1926, aged 68 years.

70 Delivery of beet to the Sugar Factory. People looking for employment waited outside the gates every day to see if there were any vacancies occurring because of sickness or absenteeism.

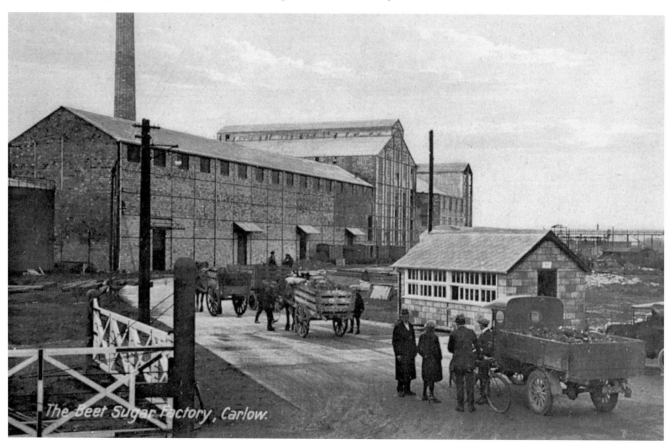

The Beet Sugar Factory, Carlow.

71 A turf cutting competition was held in 1935 at Rossmore Bog, a short distance from Carlow town. First prize was £5 won by Jack Lowry of Clogrennan. Second prize, one pound of tobacco, was won by Michael Farrell of Rossmore. Third prize, a slane, was won by Joe Toole of Rossmore. At the upper left of the picture we see, with white beard, Mick 'The Wiseacre' Malone of Rossmore chatting with the historian priest Fr. Peadar MacSuibhne. Having a smoke behind them are Dr. Lane, Medical Officer, Ballickmoyler and Fr. Edward Campion. The event was organized by the Turf Co-operative Committee, the secretary was Liam Bolton. Following the competition a tug-o-war was held between Rossmore turf cutters and the Clogrennan lime burners. Also included in the picture are Joe Toole, Jack Lowery and three Jim Dunnes – from three generations of the same family.

72 In volume 1 picture number 63 we saw a large group of eminent citzens assembled at the Town Hall preparing to leave for the laying of the foundation stone of Killeshin Water-works. In the scene pictured here we see that they have arrived. The ceremony was performed by Michael Governey. Copies of newspapers and some gold, silver and copper coins were sealed in the cavity of the foundation stone. Local women and children, some in bare feet, witness the cermony.

73　One of my favourite pictures, it could be captioned 'Spot the nun'. On what appears to be a bitterly cold day we see sixteen members of the teaching and nursing religious order of Mercy nuns pictured on their annual outing to Killeshin Waterworks four miles from their convent. Most of them seem anxious to shelter along the wall of the reservoir. Despite the gloomy looking atmosphere, Sister Fidelis (pictured third from the left) tells me that this outing was a great treat. The twigs and branches are gathered and piled to make a fire for the ensuing picnic.

74 I include this picture because up to the late 1960's emigration was part of Irish life. Many of those who left for the USA did well for themselves, but some of them never returned. With jugs of beer and bottles of wine on the table and a bottle of whiskey underneath, most of those pictured are from Carlow, attending a Carlow dance in the early 1950's in New York City. They are (1. to 14.): Har Clarke, Eliz Clarke, Mike Murphy, M. McGrath, E. Gallagher, Kathleen Mulvey, Denis O'Neill, Mary Carroll, S. Gallagher, Maureen Reynolds, Dolly Reynolds, John Snoddy, Pat Lennon and Mary Montgomery. Kathleen Mulvey emigrated to New York in 1929 and in the following years helped many later arrivals. She is Honorary President of the Carlow County Heritage Society. In 1999 Kathleen was the recipient of the 'Carlovian of the Century Award' and deserves a special mention in this volume.

75   The Church of St. Mary's is the third structure on the same site. The church records date back to 1669 and contain interesting details concerning life in Carlow down through the centuries. One such entry states that in 1746 John Clarke was appointed at a salary of £5 by the church committee *to discover where the large amount of illicit spirits was being manufactured and to bring the guilty culprits to justice.* It appears that his search was successful because, a short time later, he reported back to the committee who noted that *he was obviously under the influence of alcohol.* He was dismissed! In 1832 the church was remodelled, widened and a new spire erected. The previous church building was much smaller with a low belfry, and was the church referred to by Dean Swift when, following a visit to Carlow, he penned the lines:

Poor Town, proud people
High Church, low steeple.

76 The famed 'Carlow Septet' were invited to sing all over Ireland. They even featured on national radio. In this picture, taken in 1936, we see, left to right: Pearse Prendergast, Billy O'Connor, Stan Reynolds and Jack Kirwan. Seated: Tom Meighan, Aidan Murray and Joe Donohue. It was reported that Tom Meighan had a perfect voice, 'beautifully placed with absolute pitch'. They were offered a contract but declined because of family and work commitments. Their signature tune was 'Gaudeamus igitur', a medieval student song with the following verse:

Let us rejoice, therefore, when we are young. After our joyful youth: after care-ridden old age: We all come to the clay.

I hope you enjoyed sharing Carlow history through the camera lens.